187 TIPS FOR ARTISTS

How to create a successful art career — and have fun in the process!

KATHY GULRICH

Library of Congress Control Number: 2003097349

ISBN 0-9746533-0-6

Center City Publishing
P.O. Box 1292
New York, NY 10156

To my mom, whose generosity and boundless energy are an inspiration to me, and to everyone around her. Love always.

CONTENTS

INTRODUCTION

Virtually every time I chat with an artist, when the subject of business comes up, I hear pretty much the same thing: "I don't know where to start," or "I really hate spending time on it."

It's not that surprising, really. Many artists who are very creative and successful at their art, get a bit overwhelmed by the business of art. And that's one of the reasons I decided to write this book.

The way I look at it, there's absolutely nothing to be overwhelmed about.

In fact, I think the business of art can actually be quite easy – if you break it down into simple steps, and get the support and encouragement you need along the way.

And I'll even take it a step further. Taking care of the business side of art doesn't mean you can't have fun. In fact, it's quite the opposite.

Once you start getting the business stuff under your belt, all that's left is fun!

Want to see for yourself? Here's my challenge:

Each day, for the next 30 days, choose just one tip from this book, and do it.

You don't need to start at the beginning. In fact, you can jump around as much as you like. Just do one action, every day, for one month. No matter which tips you choose, I'm willing to bet you'll be a much happier – and much more successful – artist!

Kathy Gulrich

SECTION 1:

Taking Care of the Basics

SPREAD *the word.*

Tell everyone you know that you're a working artist – not just someone "who happens to do art." Let them know your work is for sale. And invite them to all your shows – whether your artwork is on the wall of your uncle's restaurant, or in a prestigious gallery.

MAKE *a small portfolio with photographs of your work.*

Granted, galleries and most juried shows want to see slides of your work. But your buddies at the office? Your neighbors and friends? They'd probably prefer photographs. So show them your artwork in a small, professional portfolio (or plain leather photo album) – 4"x 6" photos are just about right.

PROTECT *your copyright.*

How? Register your artwork with the United States Library of Congress. It's easy. And it's necessary – especially if you're showing or selling your work online. You'll find all the information you need – including downloadable PDF forms – at the U.S. Copyright Office: http://www.loc.gov/copyright

NAME *your paintings.*

Do you want to own a painting named "untitled?" I certainly don't. Give your paintings titles that your buyers can respond to. Use titles that will make them smile, help them understand your thoughts, or tune into the emotion of the piece more quickly and easily. Titles help your collectors relate to your work, and show them how much you care about each painting.

UPDATE *your resume after every show.*

Okay, I admit it. It happened to me. One of my friends offered to take a packet of my materials to one of her gallery-owner friends – and when I sat down to print out fresh copies, I noticed that my most recent shows were not on my resume! Learn from my mistake – and update your resume after every show.

COMPILE *an "annotated" resume.*

Unlike your artist resume (for galleries and shows), an annotated resume is for your use only – and includes all available information about your shows: title of the show; gallery address, phone/fax, curator's name, affiliation, address, commission percentages, artwork you exhibited (including size, medium, price), any work sold, etc. It's an efficient – and easy – way to keep all your show information in one place.

WRITE *your bio.*

You can do it in less than an hour if you write just a sentence or two that answers each of these questions: How did you get started? What are you doing now (broad view)? What's your work all about (medium, technique, etc.)? What are your major accomplishments (awards, articles, recognitions) so far? Where did you study, and what degrees do you hold? That's it. Do it now!

PREPARE *a short bio with your photo.*

Your short bio should include a quick summary of your longer bio (in larger, easy-to-read type), a photo (to make it more personal), and your contact information. Put it inside a transparent page sleeve to keep it clean, and attach it to your portfolio, or to any print stands where you display your work.

COLLECT *artist statements from five of your artist friends.*

I've never met an artist who said they actually enjoyed writing their artist statement. Yet every professional artist I know has written one. To get some inspiration – and possibly a good chuckle – while writing yours, ask your friends to share theirs with you before you get started.

WRITE *an artist statement that's low on "fluff," and high on what makes your work unique.*

Take a stab at your artist statement by writing down every phrase you can think of that describes your work. Think color, technique, shape, size – and write whatever comes to mind. Add in some ideas about how you view your work; what makes you tick. Then – and this is the most important part – cross out at least half of the adjectives. What's left is probably a pretty good first draft!

TALK *to your accountant or tax consultant now.*

Don't wait until a few weeks before tax time. Ask now what may be deductible on your next tax return, and what records or receipts you need to save. Next April, it'll be much easier to file, and get all the deductions you're entitled to.

DECIDE *whether to price your artwork framed, matted, or unframed.*

If how your artwork is framed is very important to you, you may want to sell your work framed. Also, works on paper often look much better framed – or nicely matted. However you decide to go, be sure to add the cost of matting and framing to the selling price!

CONSIDER *pricing your artwork according to size.*

Price your artwork by size, and your pricing will be really clear and easy for your customers to understand. And you'll save lots of time on pricing when you add new work to your portfolio – because based on size, you'll already know what it costs. That said, you may want to group your paintings by medium or technique – and price the groupings differently. Within each grouping, though, consider the "price by size" rule.

TYPE *out a price list that includes every piece of your work.*

Yes, write down a price for every piece in your studio! Then, next time someone asks you how much one of your pieces costs, you won't stutter and squirm (as I did my first couple of months...). You'll be able to answer confidently, and will be well on your way to selling your work!

STICK *to your prices no matter what.*

If a gallery customer gets a lower price from you than from the gallery, the gallery will get angry (and may drop you). And if you discount for a friend, they're probably thinking someone else got an even better deal, so they're not totally happy anyway – and you get less than your work is worth. Never discount your artwork. Not to friends, not to family. Never.

KEEP *your pricing consistent. Everywhere.*

Say one of your best collectors, who just bought one of your paintings in New York for $1,000, heads to Utah on vacation. While there, he sees another of your paintings, in the same series, retailing for just $600. What happens to your relationship with that collector? Enough said.

CREATE *a professional-looking business card and give it out often.*

Feel free to include a photo of your artwork on your card – if it reproduces well and is representative of your work. Also include your name, address (studio or home), telephone, e-mail, and website address. With the right card, people will remember you and your art – and will have all the information they need to contact you to purchase your art.

CARRY *at least a dozen business cards with you at all times.*

Do you ever notice that when one person asks for your card, suddenly others do, too? Don't be caught short! With a dozen cards in your pocket, you'll never have to say, "Sorry, that was my last card."

CREATE *a business letterhead and use it for all your art-related correspondence.*

Unless you have an uncle in the printing business, you may want to create a simple letterhead on your computer. It might include your name and type of artwork in fairly large type on the top of the page, centered. All your contact information might be centered on the bottom, below a rule that separates it from the text. If you're not comfortable designing it yourself, ask someone to help you.

HIRE *a professional photographer to shoot your artwork.*

Most often, galleries and shows request slides of your work, rather than the original artwork. So make sure your slides are fabulous! Unless you know you can do a superb job yourself, hire a professional photographer to shoot your work. Not just any photographer, however. Be sure you find one who has experience shooting artwork for slides (ask your artist friends for recommendations).

ASK *your photographer to shoot — and give you — two original slides of your artwork.*

The first original slide is for your permanent record, and never leaves your file. (Yes, I said never.) The second original is the slide you use to make duplicate slides (known as "dupes") that you will send out to galleries and shows.

WRITE *a business plan.*

Treat your art as a business, and you're much more likely to earn a profit from it. Get off to a great start by writing a business plan that includes, at a minimum: your product, your goals, time frame (1, 2 or 5 year outlook), how you plan to market your work, and your budget (income and outflow). Do an online search for "writing business plan" and you'll find several free guides.

WRITE *down what you'd like to accomplish over the next six months, and over the next year.*

Make sure you write goals that are specific, realistic, and achievable. For example, rather than writing "I'm going to start selling my artwork," you might write, "I will sell one painting a month from now until June, and two paintings a month starting July."

TELL *the world where you're heading!*

Over and over, research has shown that people who tell others about their goals are more successful at achieving them. So don't keep your goals to yourself.

BE *yourself with the basics.*

Yes, you should prepare totally professional artist materials (resume, bio, artist statement, etc.). Remember, though, that "professional" and "stodgy" are not synonymous! Make sure you bring a big dose of "you" into your artist materials.

TAKING CARE OF THE BASICS

SECTION 2:

Getting Off to a Great Start

GET *started.*

Too often, artists want to have everything "perfect" before they start to show their work. Perfect paintings, perfect technique, perfect framing, perfect studio, etc. Do you really think your work will ever be perfect? My point exactly. So get started. Now.

REMOVE *the words "starving artist" from your vocabulary. Immediately!*

Nope. I'm not even going to say anything about it. Get it right out of your head! Out! Not another mention. Ever.

WRITE *down your definition of success.*

If you don't know what success is – for you – how will you know when you get there? Before midnight tomorrow, write down how you define success: money? (if so, how much?) fame? selling your work? (how many pieces?) having more time for your family? having more time to paint? getting a solo show in a gallery? having more fun? Be specific!

KEEP *a written record of how much you spend — on what — for at least two weeks.*

Most people who write down all their expenses for two weeks find a surprise or two. So why not give it a try? Write down everything you spend money on: newspapers, coffee, transportation, gifts, whatever. Then multiply each week's total by 52 to figure out what you're spending in a year on that particular item. Take a look. Any spending habits you'd like to change?

CREATE *a budget that will allow you to continue to do art for as long as you like.*

A budget is not as hard as you think. You just need to take a look – on paper – at how much money is coming in, and how much money is going out. Be sure you save part of what you earn in the good times to get you through any tough times that may come your way.

PUT *together a mailing list of everyone you know.*

Today, you might not have any news to announce. But you will! So starting right now, compile a mailing list of all your contacts – friends, colleagues, relatives, neighbors, fellow artists, medical/tax professionals, etc. – so you'll have it ready to go when you do have something to say. Hint: Collect names and telephone numbers plus snail- and e-mail addresses.

DOCUMENT *your process.*

Keeping really good records will save you lots of time – and frustration. Which two colors did you mix to make that perfect purple? How much extra water did you add to the plaster? What did you add to the medium to get that terrific crackly finish? What's the name of the company that stocks the special hand-made paper you love? Write it all down!

TAKE *photos of your work in progress.*

While you're working on a project, stop every now and then to take a snapshot of your work in progress. Later, it'll be much easier for you to explain – or show – how you work.

REMEMBER *Thomas Edison's* *"99% perspiration, 1% inspiration."*

It may be pretty old, but it's still worth taking to heart. Being a successful artist is more than creativity and "inspiration." If you really want to be successful, don't forget to add in a good dose of hard work.

CONGRATULATE *yourself* *on all your "firsts."*

Write down every "first" as it happens. Your first framed painting. Your first out-of-state customer. Your first online show. Your first oil painting. Take a few minutes to update your list every week. You'll be happy to have it to re-read on those inevitable "low" days.

USE *the power of the Internet.*

Go online to gather information about upcoming shows and exhibitions, to research galleries, and to find out what other artists are up to. You can get information about art in your city – or anywhere else in the world – almost instantaneously.

TAKE *advantage of free e-stuff.*

There's an incredible amount of terrific information available on the Internet – just for the asking. Start by getting your free smART business e-newsletter – filled with valuable tips, articles, and ideas for artists. Sign up now at: www.smARTbusinessCoaching.com

LET *people know what makes you unique.*

Figure out what it is that makes you – and your work – unique. Then let your potential customers – whether individuals, shows, or galleries – know about it. It could be a special technique, subject matter, or material. Or maybe how you think about your work, or why you became an artist. People like to know what makes you YOU!

JOT *down prices of other artists' work.*

Whether you've already priced your work or not, knowing what other artists are charging is one good way to determine (or adjust) your selling price. So jot down prices wherever – and whenever – you see your fellow artists selling work.

GO *the extra mile.*

Little things often make a big difference. Examples? You could hand-deliver your work to the gallery instead of shipping it. Or share one of your "secret" techniques with a fellow artist. Come up with your own ideas – and make a habit of using them.

WRITE *an article about your work for your local newspaper.*

Getting free press is a great way of letting people in your area know about you, and your work. If writing is not your strong suit, ask a friend to help. Or create something newsworthy, and ask if one of the staff writers of your local newspaper would like to interview you.

HANG *your own artwork in your house or apartment.*

Displaying your work at home reminds everyone who visits that you're an artist, and you're proud of your work. It can be a great way to sell your artwork, too. (I've sold several paintings right off the wall to friends and collectors who stopped by for dinner – or a studio visit!)

FIND *at least one new way to exhibit your work that doesn't rely on galleries and shows.*

Ask a friend to hang your work at an upcoming party or business gathering. Add your work to a group website. Make artwork t-shirts for friends and family. Hang your work at a local coffee shop. Make it into personal note cards or postcards. Do whatever you can to get your work out there!

SHOWCASE *your artwork on your own art website.*

If you have good quality slides, photographs, or digital files of your artwork – and your resume, bio, and artist statement – you have everything you need for your first website. Whether you create it yourself, hire a web designer, or get help from a friend, keep it simple. Unless it's your creative medium, don't use "flash," wild backgrounds, slow-loading intros – or anything else that will detract from your work.

BE *yourself from the start.*

Yes, you should present yourself in a professional manner every time you show someone your work. But never try to be someone you're not. Let your personality come through, and you'll be the best business person you can be: you!

SECTION 3:

Getting Your Artwork into Galleries and Shows

DO *your homework.*

You'll get fewer rejections – and spend a lot less money – if you check out shows and galleries before you submit your work. Things to look for: the type of work they usually select (e.g., photorealism vs. experimental), previous show winners, the curator's website or bio, artists represented by the gallery, prices of artwork sold in the gallery, and so on. If your work doesn't fit, don't send it.

VISIT *art galleries as a customer – rather than an artist.*

This way, you can check out how the gallery routinely treats visitors (your future customers and collectors). And you'll learn first-hand how they promote – or don't promote – their artists' work.

CHECK *out at least one gallery a week.*

The best way to get your work into a gallery is to find the gallery that's perfect for your work. So check out at least one gallery every week until you find five galleries where you think your work would fit in, and look great.

SAY *"no" to vanity galleries.*

A vanity gallery is one that charges you to hang your work. They might charge a lump sum, say, $1,000 for a one-week show. Or they might charge membership fees (cost to join, then monthly fees) that guarantee you a show within a certain time period. Unless you have money to burn, avoid these vanity galleries. Most critics and reviewers do.

CONTACT *an artist represented by a gallery that interests you.*

Chatting with an artist about a gallery will give you much more information than you could ever get meeting with the gallery owners. Is the gallery easy to work with? Do they stand behind their agreements? How quickly do they pay the artist for work sold?

USE *reputable sources* *to find information about shows and galleries.*

How do you know which sources are best? Go for the larger, more established lists and publications. Ask your artist friends where they get their information. And most importantly, trust your gut. If it doesn't feel right, don't do it.

FOLLOW *show entry rules completely—and exactly!*

There's a lot of competition for the best shows and exhibitions. Give yourself the best chance possible by being meticulous about filling out the forms, labeling your slides, and including all requested materials. Check and double-check your entry before you send it out.

INCLUDE *a cover letter with every show entry form you mail.*

Format might include: 1) I'm happy for this opportunity, 2) Here's why I've selected this particular work, and why it's perfect for the show, 3) I've enclosed (everything they've asked for, and maybe something extra), and 4) Again, I appreciate this great opportunity, and look forward to hearing the results.

KEEP *all your completed show entry forms in one file folder, in order by date.*

Two months before each show date next year, decide if you want to re-apply to the show – and if so, request the new entry form. It will be much easier to fill out the new form with the old one as reference!

REMEMBER *that galleries and shows do not reject you.*

It may feel like they're rejecting you. But they're not. When a show or gallery doesn't accept your work, it simply means that they've decided to show different work. Not better work. Not more exciting work. Not more creative work. Just different work. It's that simple.

GET *your gallery agreements in writing.*

Two pieces of advice here. First, never sign anything without fully understanding it – and agreeing to all its provisions. And second, if a gallery you'd like to work with doesn't have a prepared document, write one, and ask for their signed agreement. Either way, remember that it's always best to consult an attorney.

CHECK *out online galleries carefully.*

While online galleries may be a good place to showcase your work, most are not (yet) very good at selling artwork. So before you submit your artwork to an online gallery, try to determine how well it will meet your objectives. And be sure to protect your copyright by registering your work with the Library of Congress before you go online!

GET *your foot in the door with small pieces.*

If you're a relatively new artist, it may be difficult to persuade a gallery to hang your work, even in a group show. So think small. Many galleries have pre-holiday group shows of "small works" – and they might be willing to include a piece or two of yours. And when they sell? Well, you know the rest....

PUT *your contact information on everything that leaves your hands. Everything!*

You'll probably remember to put your contact information on your resume, artist statement, cover letters, etc. Don't forget to put it on your paintings, note cards, show announcements, invitations, thank-you notes, and so on. Make it super-easy for potential collectors to find you.

SHOW *more work, more often.*

Can you get your work into four shows this year? How about a show every month? Or at least one piece, somewhere, every week of the year? Aim high. Be really creative about how – or where – you can show your work. And get it out there as often as possible.

HOST *a studio open house to show your friends, collectors, and future collectors your newest work.*

Notice I didn't say "art sale" or "studio sale." Every now and then it's great to let people see what you're up to without the pressure of buying. Invite everyone you know, and have a ball.

DONATE *a piece of artwork to your favorite charity.*

This is nothing short of a win-win-win situation! Your charity gets a piece of artwork to hang – or to sell for a much-needed contribution. And you win twice. You get the satisfaction of helping your favorite charity, and get your work seen by an entirely new audience.

INVITE *people to your next show – even if you know they can't attend.*

Remember, the purpose of your invitation is not only to get people to attend your show. It's also to let people know that you're out there showing your work – being a successful artist.

ATTEND *every one of your show and gallery openings.*

Make it a point to show up to meet guests, meet collectors and potential collectors, meet other artists, and make connections. (And, of course, be totally proud and have fun!)

BE *yourself with galleries and shows.*

If you're in art for the long term, resist doing artwork you think "they" want. Instead, do what's right for you. I must confess, I actually did an oil painting of a rooster for a show I entered (hey, they didn't have a "human" category, and almost all my work is figural!). But I would not be very happy doing roosters every week – no matter how well they sold.

SECTION 4:

Building Relationships with Your Customers and Collectors

INVITE *your customers inside your head.*

Art collectors are almost always curious about how you create – so find ways to share your process with them. You might invite them to an informal demo. Show them photographs of the location that inspired you. Or if possible, let them try the process themselves!

BE *a collector yourself.*

Here are three good reasons: You'll know first-hand how your collectors feel when they purchase your work. You'll be a great model for them. And you'll be supporting other artists.

SEND *your new collectors home with an "artist pack."*

When new collectors pick up your artwork, be sure to give them an "artist pack" – a professional-looking folder with your business card, resume, artist statement, bio, articles, etc. You'll be amazed at how many of their friends and associates will see it!

LET *your customers be excited about their purchase.*

Remember that when you sell a painting, it's also an exciting event for the buyer! So when they compliment you or your work, accept the compliment graciously, say "thank you," and be totally professional. This is not the time for modesty.

LET *your buyers know you're excited about the sale.*

Share something personal that lets your buyers know that you're excited about the sale, too. Tell them how the sale is meaningful to you: your first, your first to someone in New Jersey, your first in this series, your last one like this, etc.

ASK *your collectors for their advice and input.*

Invite your best collectors to your studio to show them new projects you're working on – and ask them what they think. They'll be flattered that you're interested in their opinions – and you just might get some fabulous input.

MAKE *a habit of listening for important dates and occasions.*

When you're chatting with a prospect or collector who mentions an important date (wife's birthday, wedding anniversary, etc.), make a mental note – and jot it down immediately after the meeting so you don't forget it.

REMEMBER *your collectors' very special occasions with an artwork gift.*

Imagine having a small piece of your artwork forever connected in your collectors' minds with their 50th anniversary, the birth of their first child, or their son's graduation from medical school. Sometimes a little goes a very long way.

EDUCATE *your customers.*

Customers who understand how you apply your paint, why you use those strange-looking long brushes, or how you get so many layers of color onto your canvas, are not only educated about what you do – they're interested in what you do. And that will translate into more sales, and more referrals.

LISTEN *more, talk less.*

It's human nature. Just about everyone would rather talk about themselves than listen to someone else. So if you're looking to make a business connection, let your customers do the talking.

LET *your customers know you're available for "commissioned" work.*

Most often, you'll sell your finished work. But a customer may "commission" a piece of artwork: ask you to do a special piece for them. It's a great opportunity for you both! Before you start, though, be sure you agree on the terms of the commission, including: size, medium, timing, and any special requests – plus price, and how payments will be made (often 40% up front, 30% midway, and 30% upon delivery).

BUILD *personal relationships with your prospects and collectors.*

Take relationships with your prospects and collectors beyond "business" – and start building personal relationships with them, as well. If appropriate, invite them to social gatherings, send a holiday card, or drop them a post-card from your favorite vacation spot.

FOLLOW *up – and follow through – with your customers.*

If you say you'll call on Tuesday, call on Tuesday. And always provide the materials or information you promised – completely, and on time.

CONTACT *each of your important customers regularly.*

No matter how much someone likes your work, they're simply not likely to re-contact you if you're not "top of mind" for them. So find something to say (announce, send, write...) to each of your prospects – and collectors – at least every couple months or so.

THANK *your collectors (and friends and fellow artists) personally when they attend one of your shows.*

Jot off an e-mail, write a quick note, make a call, or thank them the next time you see them. But do find a way to thank people for showing up for you.

INVITE *your customers to a sneak preview.*

If you've just finished a new series or collection – or you're ready to hang a new gallery show – invite your best customers to your studio for a special preview of your new work. They'll love it.

ATTACH *a personalized tag to the back of each of your framed paintings.*

On the tag, be sure to include the title of the painting and medium, along with your name, and how to contact you (website or e-mail address) to see – or purchase – more of your work. If you have a "logo," use it.

CLOSE *your mouth.*

Sometimes the best way to close a sale is to close your mouth. Don't keep "selling" after your customer has already decided to buy your work!

MIND *your manners!*

Remember those things your mom taught you as a kid? Like “please” and “thank you?” They still work. So use them – often.

BE *yourself with your customers and collectors.*

Yes, you may meet a collector or two who wants to be dazzled by art double-talk and rhetoric. Most collectors, however, will want to get to know the real you. They'll totally love hearing about how you work, how you feel about your artwork, some of your artistic quirks – and even some of the mistakes you've made.

SECTION 5:

Developing a Supportive Artist Community

TELL *someone you've just met that you're an artist.*

This works especially well if you're an artist who also happens to have a job doing something else. Get in the habit of telling people that you're an artist first. Wait until later in the conversation to tell them how else you describe yourself – a teacher, waiter, mother, investment banker, etc.

KICK *out limiting beliefs (along with the artists who hold them).*

"Art is too risky." "It's too late to start." "Artists never make any money." "You've got to suffer to make real art." Need I go on? Replace your limiting beliefs – and limiting friends – with more expansive ones, and watch your life change!

CELEBRATE *your successes.*

Be sure you celebrate all of your successes – and your friends' successes, too. Whether it's an award at a prestigious show, or a personalized rejection letter instead of the usual form letter, there's reason to celebrate – with a card, a kiss, a phone call, or a party.

TURN *off the TV and call an artist.*

Next time you're just hanging out with the TV, turn it off, and call an artist friend. You can be sure you'll get a whole lot more out of chatting with – or hanging out with – another artist. You'll have more fun, too.

PICK *your friends' brains.*

Even if you're just starting out and think you know absolutely nothing about marketing yourself and your work, you'll be amazed at how many good marketing ideas you and your artist friends can come up with. Get together over a cup of coffee or hot chocolate, and let the ideas fly.

LOOK *up one artist every week.*

Take a dusty art book off the shelf, go online, or ask a friend for a suggestion. Every week, learn something new about one new (to you) artist. It'll take you just a few minutes. And in a year, you'll know something interesting about more than 50 artists.

SET *up a weekly date with another artist.*

Check out a new gallery. Visit a museum. Shop for art supplies. Paint together in a park. It really doesn't matter what you decide to do – just do it every week. It'll do you both a world of good.

INTRODUCE *yourself to at least one fellow artist at every show you attend.*

Art shows can be incredibly boring – or fun and interesting. It's up to you. One way to enjoy yourself at an opening or show is to make it a point to introduce yourself to at least one other artist. Want more fun? Chat with two!

SURPRISE *an artist friend with a rose at their next show opening.*

It'll only take you an extra few minutes to pick up that rose. And it'll make the artist's day.

BUY *a piece of artwork from a beginning artist.*

Remember how great it felt the first time you sold a painting? Give that great feeling to someone else by purchasing a piece of art you love.

BRAINSTORM *regularly with your artist friends.*

Brainstorm about art, finding studio space, tracking down bargains on art supplies, writing your resume, choosing art for your business card, etc. Whatever you discuss, you'll learn a lot – and get the benefit of your friends' creative perspective.

TRADE *a piece of artwork with an artist whose work you admire.*

If you love the work of another artist, but your budget doesn't stretch far enough for a purchase, ask if they'd be willing to consider a trade. This is often a great way to add to both of your collections.

SHARE *information about upcoming art opportunities with all your artist friends.*

Contrary to what some artists seem to believe, sharing information about galleries, competitions, and other art opportunities is not just a terrific way to build the artist community – it's a fabulous way to build your own career.

SUPPORT *an emerging artist by attending their show.*

If you've ever attended an opening where there were only a few guests, you'll know how much your attendance at a show will be appreciated by a new artist. Think of the impact you could make by attending just one new artist's show or exhibition a month.

MAKE *a list of ten artists you know.*

After you've made your list, think of one thing you could do for each of them. Then pick at least three things, and do them!

CALL *an artist friend and ask them to tell you what they like most about your artwork.*

It will surely make you feel better about your work. And it may well point out something interesting in your work that you never noticed yourself.

SAY *something nice about another artist's work.*

When you pass on your compliment, be specific. "I love the way you use line" or "the purple highlights in the sky are beautiful" will be more appreciated than a simple "nice painting." However you phrase your compliment, the other artist will feel great – and so will you.

WRITE *a handwritten note telling an artist whose work you admire what you most like about it.*

Have you ever gotten a note from another artist telling you how much they like your work? Would you like to get one? So would they. Write it now.

INVITE *three friends to your studio. Play!*

The key here is to have fun. Work with new or unusual materials. Do a group project. Try a totally new technique. Make an art gift for an artist friend who couldn't join you. Anything goes, as long as it's not too serious.

BE *yourself with other artists.*

When you're dealing with galleries, show juries, customers, and collectors, you may need to lean a bit toward your "professional" side. But you can let it all hang out with your artist friends. Make sure they get to see – and appreciate – the "real" you.

SECTION 6:

Organizing Your Studio — and Yourself

KEEP *your cat away from your palette.*

Do you have any idea how big a mess can be made by just four tiny, paint-covered cat paws? Let's hope you never find out! Find a way to protect your art supplies – and artwork – from pets, from kids, and from anyone else who has a habit of nosing around your studio.

USE *a reminder service*
— so you'll always remember important dates.

Today, virtually every Internet Service Provider (ISP) has a free reminder service. Find the reminder service on yours, and use it. There's no excuse for forgetting an important date!

MAKE *a "tickler file."*

One of the easiest ways to keep track of deadlines is to write them on single sheets of notebook paper (or file cards) and then put them in a file folder in chronological order – by deadline. Then each Monday, simply check your "tickler file" folder to see what's due that week.

CREATE *a filing system that works for you.*

To start, you might want to have just a handful of folders: upcoming show entries, art tips and techniques, gallery information, resume, artist statement, etc. As you collect more information, add more folders. Whatever you do, keep it simple.

KEEP *an "idea file" that will capture and save even the tiniest snippets of ideas for another day.*

Often there's an idea – or germ of an idea – that doesn't seems to warrant its own separate "home" in your file cabinet. That's what your "idea file" is all about. Just jot it down, pop it in.

REMOVE *one useless item from your art studio every week.*

And if you've just said, "There's nothing in my studio that I don't use," remove two useless items this week! Whether it's an extra pair of scissors, a staple gun that no longer works, or wire that's the wrong size for hanging your current work, get rid of it. Now. Keep up the weekly "toss" for three months, and you'll be totally amazed at how your studio is transformed.

USE *the "rule of three" for art supplies.*

If you haven't used it in three years, offer it to an artist friend who will!

ORGANIZE *your art supplies so you don't inadvertently buy something you already have.*

Haven't we all done it? Bought new tubes of paint, containers of acrylic medium, or sheets of mounting board – only to find that we had it all along? Keep your art supplies well organized, easily accessible, and in order, and it won't happen again.

BUY *in bulk.*

Ask your art supplier if you can get a discount by buying in bulk. You'll be amazed at how often retailers will say "yes". Hint: If your art supplies aren't yet well organized, buying in bulk could actually cost you money, since you'd be stocking up on items you already have.

TAKE *advantage of sales.*

Art supply stores often have fabulous sales at the end of each semester, when they need to make room for the next semester's supplies – and in summer, when students are away. Keep your eyes open, and save.

GO *fishing.*

Whatever it takes, protect your creative time (and space) from interruptions. Unplug your phone. Lock the door. Or get a sign for your studio that lets people know when you don't want to be disturbed. "Gone Fishing" could actually work quite well.

THROW *out every magazine that has a cover date more than two months old.*

If you haven't had time to read this month's magazines, what makes you think you'll find time for this month's and last month's, too? Chances are you never will. Drop them off at your local library, or a nearby nursing home. You'll have much less clutter – and a much better chance of reading the new magazines when they come in.

STORE *your slides in two separate three-ring binders.*

In one binder, store your first set of originals – and put them somewhere you'll never be tempted to use them! The second binder is for your second originals. Remember that whenever you need to make a dupe, these second originals are the slides to take to the photo finisher.

BACK-UP *your computer files at least once a month.*

The best back-up is saving your files to disk (once a week would be fabulous!). Backing up by keeping a paper copy can work, too – but only if you make it a habit to print out all new documents you write or edit, and keep them in a file where you can find them easily.

HANG *a large manila envelope on the wall near your front door.*

Drop in all your art-related receipts as soon as you get home. Then next year, at tax time, you'll have all your art expenses in one, convenient place.

STAND *in line at the post office – less often.*

Bring your standard presentation pack (mailing envelope, folder, cover letter, slides, resume, etc.) to the post office and find out how much it costs to mail. Buy stamps for at least ten packages. Then, the next time you need to mail out a package, you can just add the stamps, and drop it in a post box.

CARRY *a pen and a tiny notebook everywhere you go.*

Suffice it to say that just having a pen and notebook in your bag isn't enough. Take it out, and use it! For ideas, names, places, phone numbers – virtually anything you're likely to forget next time you want it.

LEARN *to frame your own work.*

Framing your own work is almost always less expensive than going to a frame shop. And even more importantly – especially when you have a last-minute show opportunity – it's usually much faster, too.

WORK *on frame-friendly paper.*

Whenever you can, work on paper that fits standard-sized frames and mats. Then, when you're ready to frame, you can fit your work into less expensive – and more readily available – frames. Note: Take the time to measure. Standard-sized pads and blocks often do not meet this criteria!

BE *yourself in your studio.*

Even if you don't ask, just about everyone you know will offer you advice on how to set up your studio or workspace. Listen, learn, and then take all the "musts" with a grain of salt. The best studio is one that reflects you. Your passion, your art, and your personality. So be yourself.

SECTION 7:

Becoming More Creative

PAINT *a self-portrait.*

Did you ever notice how all the books on famous artists include the artist's self-portrait? Why wait? Do yours now!

THROW *out an hour's worth of drawings.*

Ever get so caught up in "doing it perfectly" that you totally lose your creativity and personal style? To free yourself up, make a decision to throw away every drawing you do during an entire hour of your next drawing session, and see what happens.

LIST *three things you like about your current work.*

Okay, now put your list somewhere you'll know to look for it next time you're bummed out about your work. And next time you're bummed out about your work, remember to take out your list!

VISIT *a thrift shop.*

Buy three things: One that's a great bargain. One that you'll use in an upcoming art project. And one that will make one of your friends laugh out loud.

MAKE *a mistake.*

If you find you're heading down the "perfection" highway, make a creativity detour by making a mistake – intentionally. Instead of the next perfect brushstroke, add one that's totally, absolutely, incredibly wrong for your painting. Wow. Doesn't that feel great?

DANCE *around your house for absolutely no reason.*

Go on – grab that favorite cassette or CD, and let it blare! Then dance around your house until you're totally out of breath, with a big grin on your face.

GET *a plant.*

And keep it alive! Learning to turn your attention away from your art will help you turn your attention toward your art when you're ready to work. Special bonus: the plant will make your studio look great, too.

TAKE *an art class.*

If you've been working alone for a while, it's probably time to get yourself – and your art – out of your studio. Call a local art school or museum, and sign up for an art class. You'll meet artists, learn something new, and maybe even have fun.

SET *aside at least two hours a week just for you.*

Where does creativity come from? You may never find out if you're overworked and harried. Find two hours a week (hey, that's only about 17 minutes a day!) to do absolutely nothing but concentrate on you. Go out, stay home. It doesn't matter. Just be sure you're the star of the show.

WEAR *pearls.*

Well, not literally! (Although you certainly could....) Head to your closet ... or jewelry box ... or attic ... and find something that makes you feel absolutely fabulous when you put it on. Wear it all day!

MAKE *faces at yourself in the bathroom mirror.*

You're right. Which mirror you use doesn't really matter for this one. Find a mirror – any mirror – and spend a few minutes making the funniest, or scariest, or craziest faces you can. (Hey, does this count as exercise?)

STEP *back from your work – often.*

It's a great way to check how your work is coming along. And it'll also give you a really neat perspective: you'll see your work from the distance most of your buyers will see it – and eventually, hang it.

LEARN *something new.*

Take a class or workshop. Watch an art video. Read a how-to book. Learn to make puff pastry. Try your hand at calligraphy. Have fun with something you've never done before.

GO *to a museum that you've never visited.*

And if you run out of new museums to visit, find a new gallery. Or new art fair. Or new....

FLIP *your paintbrush upside down.*

Now, with bristles up, paint at least a dozen strokes – yes, on the painting you're currently working on – with the pointy wooden end.

OPEN *your toolbox.*

Yep, the toolbox with the hammer in it. Look for something that has an interesting shape ... or that's made of a cool material ... or that just catches your eye. Then take it back to your studio and paint with it.

TAKE *a 24-hour break from doing artwork.*

You heard me – absolutely NO painting or sketching or drawing or sculpting for at least one full day! You'll be amazed at how differently you approach your work when you get back to it the following morning.

DIG *out some of the artwork you did more than a year ago.*

Ever look at your old work and wonder why you ever thought it was any good at all? No matter how different – or how much "better" – you think your work is today, there's something to be learned from your older paintings or drawings. So go find a couple of pieces, and hang out with them until you find at least one thing you still love about each of them.

HOLD *one of your paintings in front of a large mirror, and check out the reflection.*

Does it look pretty good? Great. Make you grimace and turn away? Could be time to check out your painting's composition or balance, and give it another go.

TEAR *one of your old drawings into 27 pieces, and use the pieces to make a collage.*

I figured out a way to make exactly 27 pieces with just 6 tears. How did you do? (If you did it with fewer tears, please write and let me know how: kathy@smARTbusinessCoaching.com) And don't forget the collage!

TURN *one of your paintings upside down.*

Upside down is often the best way to get the right answers to what's "just not right" with your painting. Whatever's not working will often jump right out at you when you take a look from down under.

SIT *down to paint if you usually stand (or stand, if you usually sit).*

It's part of my "shake it up" theory. You – and your art – will both be more interesting if you do something differently once in a while.

GET *a massage.*

Not because your shoulders are so tight they're stuck up next to your ears. Not because your back is aching. Not because you had a crazy week. Get a massage just because it's a fabulous day, and you totally deserve one!

GIVE *a massage.*

Isn't there someone in your life who could use a nice back or neck massage? Even if you're not a pro, chances are they'd be pleased if you surprised them with one!

CLOSE *your eyes and sketch a self-portrait.*

That's right. Don't look at your face. Don't look at your paper. Just draw. Hint: If you tape your paper to a sturdy support, you can use your non-drawing hand to feel the contours of your face while you're drawing.

GET *up two hours earlier than usual, and draw or paint before you fully wake up.*

Few things kill creativity faster than getting sidetracked by detail. So this tip makes attention to detail virtually impossible. Roll out of bed ... grab your materials ... and go! No planning, no thinking, no judging, no second-guessing. Just see where your creativity takes you.

SWITCH *hands next time you start a drawing.*

If you're right-handed, draw with your left hand; if left-handed, draw with your right.

FIND *a kid.*

Picasso once said, "Every child is an artist. The problem is how to remain an artist after one grows up." To re-awaken the creativity you had as a child, find a kid, and let him or her teach you something about art.

TAKE *a walk.*

I'm sure you know the physical benefits of walking. Don't forget the mental benefits – like re-focusing your attention, getting un-stuck, and jogging your creativity.

PAINT *in your head.*

Display an unfinished painting where you'll pass it several times a day. Don't paint, just look. Again, and again. No brushes, no paint. Just "paint in your head." After a week or so, bring the painting back to your studio. You'll be totally amazed at how quickly it will move forward.

DO *some art today – even if you don't feel like it.*

In fact, do some art today especially if you don't feel like it! You don't need to spend the day, an hour – or even 10 minutes – working in your studio. Wherever you are, just do one "art" thing for a minute or so.

READ *a trashy novel.*

Or a travel magazine. Or a book on feng shui. Just about anything that transports you away from your artwork for a while will result in better artwork. Try it!

PUT *on your jammies in the middle of the day.*

Then set the alarm, and take a big old nap. (No, lying down on the couch for half an hour does not count! If there are no jammies, and there's no alarm clock, it's not a nap in my book!)

EMBARRASS *yourself.*

Don't get me wrong. I'm not suggesting you deliberately go out there and embarrass yourself. What I am suggesting, though, is that you go out there willing to embarrass yourself if that's what it takes to share your art, or yourself, with the world.

BE *yourself with your artwork.*

Some people say you have to choose: do what you love, or do what sells. I say, "do what you love." Period. You'll have a fabulous time whether your work sells or not. (And I'd be willing to bet that if your work is really "you," it will sell.)

BECOMING MORE CREATIVE

SECTION 8:

Just Good Common Sense!

WORK *hard at your art.*

Even great marketing won't be successful if your artwork isn't your best. So fine-tune your skills, experiment with new materials and techniques, and learn as much as you can – everywhere. Constantly strive to improve your work.

WRITE *thank-you notes to three people who have helped you become a better artist.*

One sentence will do it. Try, "Thanks for cheering me up when I was really bummed out about the show rejection," or "Thanks for helping me with the framing – I couldn't have done it without you," or "Thanks for showing me how to use those oil pastels – I'm having lots of fun with them." Now that didn't take very long, did it?

LISTEN *to your gut.*

Chances are you've had at least one bad experience, and afterwards, said something like, "I knew that would happen. I just felt it." Next time, listen to your gut before you make your move. Your "feel" on the situation is almost always right.

SIMPLIFY *your life.*

Clear out a closet. Streamline your studio. Eliminate commitments that don't make you happy. You'll have more time for art – and the things that matter to you most.

SPLURGE *on a bouquet of flowers.*

Bring them home, or find a spot for them in your studio. And find a few minutes – every couple of hours – to thoroughly enjoy them. Each time you do, give yourself a pat on the back for being smart enough to buy them!

CREATE *abundance in your life.*

There are lots of ways to create abundance in your life. My favorite? Be generous. With your time, with yourself, with your stuff.

LAUGH *a lot.*

Yep, laughing has actually been proven to help healing. And I even read one study that claimed that laughing could help you lose weight – since you burn calories having a good belly laugh! Don't know if I believe that one. But I do believe that laughing and smiling will make being an artist much more fun. What do you think?

TAKE *care of yourself.*

Yep, you'll feel better if you eat well, get some sleep, and exercise at least now and then. Remember, too, to check in with your doctor and dentist once in a while. You won't be able to do your best work if you're not feeling well.

GET *health insurance.*

If you're not eligible for health insurance through your job, or spouse, find an affordable plan for yourself. Ask your friends for resources, or contact your local or state art organizations to find out about available plans.

DO *something scary.*

No, you don't have to start by parachuting out of a plane (although you could!). You might start by introducing yourself to a gallery owner, telling someone the price of your painting, or asking a question in an art class. Just decide what you're going to do – and do it.

SPEND *within your budget.*

You came up with your budget so that you could continue doing art as long as you like, right? Remind yourself of that fact every single time you're tempted to spend more than you've budgeted for. And don't overspend.

REMOVE *"if" from your vocabulary.*

"I'll do it if the gallery calls" "I'll finish it if I can get someone to help me." "I'll bring it over if I'm not too tired after the show." How many "if"s do you use in a typical day? Try replacing "if" with "now" (for example, "I'll do it now.") – and see how dramatically your life changes.

ASK *for what you want.*

Don't expect your friends (or colleagues, or gallery contacts, or customers, for that matter) to be mind readers. If you want or need something, ask for it. You'll quadruple your chances of getting what you want!

SHOW *up on time.*

If you can't show up on time, show up early. It's just common courtesy. And makes good business sense, too.

ASK *for a discount.*

Many art supply chains offer a standard 10-15% discount to art students – but only if you ask for it. So if you're taking art courses, bring your student ID along every time you shop for supplies. Not a student? Don't let that stop you. Speak to the manager of the store you most often use for art supplies (or frames, or office supplies, or...), and see if you can work something out.

WRITE *down ten things you're grateful for.*

Right now. If your list starts out pretty quickly, then slows near seven or eight, all the more reason to stick with it until you reach ten. Do it every day – before you get out of bed in the morning, or last thing before you go to sleep. Try it for a week, and see what happens.

MAKE *a decision.*

Whether you're doing a painting, figuring out which juried shows to enter, or choosing an art instructor, you'll have several options. Take a bit of time to look at your choices, and then make a decision. The only decision that's sure to be wrong, is making no decision.

MAKE *a difference.*

Often the best contribution you can make is you. Find ways to donate your talents – or your time – wherever, and whenever, you can. You really can make a difference.

TURN *your attention from what's not working, to what is.*

Look for it, and you'll always find something negative or unpleasant in your life. So, why look for it? Instead, look for what is working, and put your attention there. You'll feel much happier, and create more positive experiences in your life.

LIVE *in the present.*

Don't waste time recreating the past, or imagining the future. There's only one moment you can truly experience, and that's the one you're in. Enjoy it!

ASK *for help when you need it.*

Sticking with something that's not working seldom gets you where you want to go. Need help or advice? Ask for it. Then show your appreciation with a sincere "thanks." Hopefully one day you'll be able to pass on some help to someone else who needs a hand.

FIX *something that's broken.*

You'd be amazed at how much attention – and energy – is pulled away from your art by something that's not working in your home or studio. It could be a broken VCR, a leaky faucet, or the broken light fixture in the basement. Take a few minutes to fix whatever's broken. Now!

SAY *"no."*

Artists who never seem to have enough time for their artwork are often artists who haven't learned to say "no." So if you want more time, say "no" more often. Try these on for size: "I'd love to, but I really don't have time." "Sorry, I can't handle that right now." "I can't help out this time." Or a simple, and effective, "No."

SAY *"yes."*

Be sure to stand up and say "yes" when you'd like to be involved. Volunteer for a committee. Help another artist with a project. Invite yourself along on a museum visit. (Hint: You'll have a lot more time to say "yes" when you've learned to say "no.")

TAKE *one small action toward your goals every day.*

Most worthwhile goals aren't achieved overnight, so it's helpful to find ways to keep your momentum going. Suggestion? Every single day, do at least one thing that will get you closer to your goal.

HAVE *fun.*

Remember when you first decided to become an artist? Was "fun" anywhere in the picture? If being an artist is becoming more work, and less fun, now is the time to do something about it!

BE *yourself!*

On the off chance that the idea hasn't quite sunk in yet, I thought I'd repeat it just once more: Be yourself. In business, in relationships, in art – and in your life. You'll be much happier. And a whole lot more successful, to boot!

I'd love to hear which tips worked best for you.
Please share your successes with me!

e-mail: kathy@smARTbusinessCoaching.com
website: www.smARTbusinessCoaching.com

ABOUT THE AUTHOR

As an artist, Kathy was a bit of a late starter. In fact, she didn't do her first painting until after her 50th birthday. But it was love at first try. And just two years later, she left her advertising career to become a full-time artist.

Over the past couple of years, Kathy has learned a lot about art, and even more about the business of art. She has sold more than 30 paintings, and had her work featured in more than 20 shows – from the Montclair Art Museum in New Jersey, to The National Arts Club in Manhattan.

When not creating her own art, Kathy coaches other artists, helping them deal with the sometimes overwhelming business of art – easily. How? She breaks it all down into simple, easy-to-follow steps – then adds her ongoing structure and support.

Her most unique coaching qualification may be that she, too, is an emerging artist. She's out there, every day, putting herself – and her artwork – on the line. And she's proven that she knows how to do it successfully – by treating art as a business.

Kathy brings nearly twenty years of experience as teacher, corporate trainer, and workshop leader to her coaching practice. And she often draws on the business skills she gained in her many years as Creative Director for leading advertising agencies in New York, Hong Kong, Singapore, and Milan.

Kathy holds a BA degree from Rutgers University, NJ, and earned her MEd from West Chester College in Pennsylvania. She is a member of the International Association of Coaches, and the owner of smART Business Coaching, New York. Most days, you'll find Kathy working out of her studio located in a beautiful 150-year-old brownstone in midtown Manhattan.

MORE GREAT TIPS FOR ARTISTS

Free e-newsletter and articles

Ready to sell your artwork? Spend more time creating art? Get great ideas, tips, and career advice delivered straight to your inbox every month. Simply sign up for your free smART business e-newsletter at:

www.smARTbusinessCoaching.com

While on the website, click on "Articles by Kathy" to read articles from previous issues.

Order additional copies of this book

To purchase books by credit card, **order online** at www.smARTbusinessCoaching.com, or simply fill out both sides of this form and fax it to 212-689-7385.

QTY	Product	Price	Total
	187 Tips for Artists: How to Create a Successful Art Career – and Have Fun in the Process!	$11.95	
	Sales Tax(NY residents add 8.5%)		
	Shipping/Handling in U.S (add $2.00 per book)		
	Total		

Card Number

Expiration Date

Circle One:

Visa MasterCard Discover

Name on Card: ____________________

Continued on reverse

Billing Address:

Street ______________________________

City ____________________ State ________ ZIP __________

Cardholder's Signature: ______________________________

Phone: ______________________________

E-mail Address: ______________________________

Shipping Address (if different from Billing Address):

Street ______________________________

City ____________________ State ________ ZIP __________

If paying by credit card, fax completed order form to 212-689-7385.
If paying by check or money order, please mail payment and order form to:
Center City Publishing
P.O. Box 1292
New York, NY 10156

Make check or money order payable to Center City Publishing.